GLOBALIZATION

Andrew J. Milson, Ph.D.
Content Consultant
University of Texas at Arlington

Acknowledgments

Grateful acknowledgment is given to the authors, artists, photographers, museums, publishers, and agents for permission to reprint copyrighted material. Every effort has been made to secure the appropriate permission. If any omissions have been made or if corrections are required, please contact the Publisher.

Instructional Consultant: Christopher Johnson, Evanston, Illinois

Teacher Reviewer: Heather Rountree, Bedford Heights Elementary School, Bedford, Texas

Photographic Credits

Cover, Inside Front Cover, Title Page ©Justin Guariglia/Corbis. **3** (bg) ©Tommy Flynn/Photonica/Getty Images. **4** (bg) ©REUTERS/Rafiqur Rahman. **6** (bg) ©REUTERS/Beawiharta. **7** (tl) ©Steve Hix/Somos Images/Corbis. **8** (bg) Mapping Specialists. **10** (bg) ©REUTERS/Christian Charisius. **11** (bl) ©Carsten Koall/Getty Images. **13** (bg) ©Sean Gallup/Getty Images. **14** (t) ©Stefano Amantini/Atlantide Phototravel/Corbis. **16** (bg) ©Franck Robichon/epa/Corbis. **17** (bl) ©REUTERS/Carlos Barria. **18** (c) ©Olaf Kowalzik/Alamy. (cr) ©AP Photo/Beatrix Stampfli. (bl) ©Paul Almasy/Corbis. (bc) ©Ingram Publishing/Superstock. **19** (b) ©Yoshikaza Tsuno/AFP/Getty Images. **21** (bg) ©Kazuhiro Nogi/AFP/Getty Images. **22** (bg) ©Chris Minihane/Alamy. **23** (tl) ©James Bedford. **24** (bg) ©Ken Banks/kiwanja.net. **27** (t) ©age fotostock/SuperStock. **28** (tr) ©David Engelhardt/Getty Images. **30** (tr) ©Sean Gallup/Getty Images. (br) ©Lester Lefkowitz/Getty Images. **31** (bg) ©Tommy Flynn/Photonica/Getty Images. (bl) ©REUTERS/Beawiharta. (br) ©Franck Robichon/epa/Corbis. (tr) ©Crocodile Images/Getty Images.

For permission to use material from this text or product, submit all requests online at www.cengage.com/permissions.

Further permissions questions can be emailed to permissionrequest@cengage.com.

Visit National Geographic Learning online at www.NGSP.com.

Visit our corporate website at www.cengage.com.

Printed in the USA.

RR Donnelley, Menasha, WI

ISBN: 978-07362-97547

13 14 15 16 17 18 19 20 21 22

10 9 8 7 6 5 4 3

CONNECTING THE GLOBE

Factory workers in Dhaka, the capital of Bangladesh, dry jeans after heavy rains. Jeans are one example of a global product.

HOW HAS GLOBALIZATION CHANGED THE WORLD?

Are you wearing blue jeans right now? You bought those jeans in the United States, but many people from around the world helped make them. Jeans are a product of globalization. **Globalization** is the way countries use technology, communication, and transportation to connect with one another. Globalization connects governments, cultures, and **economies**, or systems of producing and distributing wealth. Globalization fuels trade and affects the way all of us live.

TRAVELING BLUE JEANS

The overall effect of globalization is to make it easier for people to make, buy, and sell goods. Take the jeans you're wearing, for example. The cotton came from the United States. In China, workers cleaned and dyed the cotton. Factories in Malaysia spun the fibers into yarn. Workers in Thailand turned the yarn into fabric. A factory in Singapore cut the cloth. The zipper was made in Hong Kong; the buttons were made in Taiwan. Indonesians sewed everything together. Back in Singapore, workers attached labels and shipped the jeans to stores around the world.

Once all the parts of the jeans are ready, they are sewn together by factory workers in Jakarta, Indonesia.

These U.S. consumers are buying jeans made in countries all over the world.

MAKING THE WORLD GO 'ROUND

Globalization is nothing new. It has been around for centuries. Nearly 2,000 years ago, Europeans traded with China and other Asian countries along a route called the Silk Road. Merchants traveled in camel caravans along segments of the Silk Road to trade their goods. In exchange for valuable silk made in China, the Europeans sent gold, silver, and goods to Asia. The trade caused each region to flourish.

Today, globalization is driven by new inventions, better communication, and countries that want to make life better for their citizens.

WHAT IS THE IMPACT?

Globalization affects everyone in different ways. For many, globalization is a positive change. It brings people of different cultures together, provides jobs to people in developing countries, and allows them to make a living. It allows businesses to make products more cheaply.

On the other hand, globalization often changes traditional ways of life. Languages may disappear and traditions may vanish. As people work to produce more products more quickly, they sometimes ignore or replace old traditions. Millions lose their jobs because the products they produce can be made more cheaply somewhere else.

In some places, globalization widens the gap between rich and poor. It can result in the misuse of **natural resources**, materials that come from the environment, such as gold, coal, or oil. It can cause the mistreatment of a country's workers. While some people prosper because of globalization, others struggle.

Explore the Issue

1. **Explain** What is globalization? Give two examples and explain why they are examples of globalization.

2. **Analyze Effects** What are two positive and two negative results of globalization?

Impact of Globa

Selected trade organizations
- European Union
- Asia-Pacific Economic Cooperation
- North American Free Trade Agreement and Asia-Pacific Economic Cooperation

UNITED STATES Globalization has caused many U.S. companies to move jobs overseas to save money. According to some, this has led to higher unemployment in the United States.

CASE STUDY 1

GERMANY Globalization has helped Germany's economy prosper. Germany now expects to have a labor shortage of 2 million workers by 2020.

SOUTH AMERICA Some believe that globalization is allowing foreign companies to use up the Amazon rain forest. Companies want to develop South America's other natural resources, such as oil and gold.

NORTH
AMERICA

NORTH
PACIFIC
OCEAN

NORTH
ATLANTIC
OCEAN

SOUTH
AMERICA

SOUTH
PACIFIC
OCEAN

SOUTH
ATLANTIC
OCEAN

Explore the Issue

1. **Interpret Maps** How are the effects of globalization different in the United States and Germany?

2. **Draw Conclusions** How has globalization affected the poverty rate in India?

ization

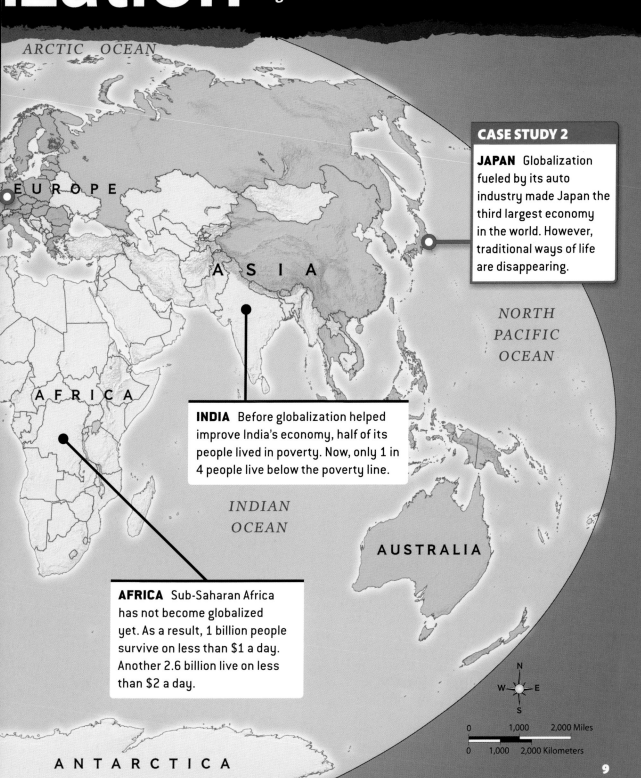

Study the map below to learn how globalization affects the world's countries.

ARCTIC OCEAN

EUROPE

ASIA

AFRICA

NORTH PACIFIC OCEAN

INDIAN OCEAN

AUSTRALIA

ANTARCTICA

CASE STUDY 2

JAPAN Globalization fueled by its auto industry made Japan the third largest economy in the world. However, traditional ways of life are disappearing.

INDIA Before globalization helped improve India's economy, half of its people lived in poverty. Now, only 1 in 4 people live below the poverty line.

AFRICA Sub-Saharan Africa has not become globalized yet. As a result, 1 billion people survive on less than $1 a day. Another 2.6 billion live on less than $2 a day.

N
W—E
S

| 0 | 1,000 | 2,000 Miles |
| 0 | 1,000 | 2,000 Kilometers |

A huge transport ship delivers only part of the enormous A380. This passenger airplane can hold 525 people in a three-class configuration or 853 people in an all-economy class configuration.

SECTION 11/13
A380
JIG No. 6

6700 kg tare

Total 35 to. Tare

EXPANDING
Germany's
Economy

BUILDING A FUTURE

What is as wide as a football field and as long as two blue whales? What weighs as much as 165 elephants and stands taller than five giraffes? Give up? It's the Airbus A380 super jumbo jet, the world's largest passenger airplane.

Frankfurt's international airport is the size of 2,000 football fields. Partly to receive the huge A380, it has already expanded. The airport has a new runway, a new terminal, and a massive new hangar that will fit two of the new A380s or three Boeing 747s.

For Germany's 81 million people, the airbus and airport are important symbols of that country's climb up the global economic ladder. After its defeat in World War II (1939–1945), Germany fought to become one of the world's richest countries. The country's rise was helped enormously by globalization.

DIVIDED COUNTRY

After the United States, Britain, France, and the Soviet Union triumphed in World War II, they divided Germany in half. East Germany became a Soviet-backed **communist** country. That meant that the state controlled everything and citizens had no private property. A doctor made the same salary as a plumber. People could not travel or speak their minds. Meanwhile, West Germany became a **democracy**, in which citizens elected representatives to run the country. In 1957, West Germany joined the European Economic Community, which was also known as the **Common Market**. This was an alliance that removed trade barriers among European countries.

Many East Germans escaped to the West, hoping to find a better life. To keep its citizens from fleeing, the East German government built a wall that divided Berlin into two parts. The wall was over 100 miles long and made of concrete. In 1989, though, the East German government collapsed. Citizens on both sides of the Berlin Wall knocked it down.

German children and artists made 1,000 Styrofoam dominoes and toppled them to celebrate the 20th anniversary of the fall of the Berlin Wall.

GERMANY ON THE RISE

The collapse of the Berlin wall was a symbol to the world that communism had failed. Germany became one country again with a unified government. For the first time in decades, Germans could move freely around the country.

At first, Germany's new united economy faltered. It was costly for the new Germany to bring the productivity and wages of workers from East Germany up to the standards of West Germany. However, things slowly improved. Factories, such as those that produced Volkswagens, buzzed with work, and good-paying jobs were plentiful. In 1993, Germany joined the **European Union (EU)**, which grew out of the Common Market. The European Union created a central European bank and a common form of money, called the **euro**. The EU supports increased world trade, which is a major benefit of globalization.

It didn't take long for Germany to become Europe's richest country and a world leader in iron, steel, and coal production. German companies also exported electronics, chemicals, and automobiles around the world. Germany created high-quality tools and machines that countries around the world use.

JOBS! JOBS! JOBS!

Germany's success led to a problem: too many jobs for too few workers. Germany's population is aging, with 20 percent of its people over the age of 65. The median age of German citizens is about 45 years old. Meanwhile the birth rate is at zero growth. Many older workers are retiring, and younger Germans cannot fill all the jobs. Experts predict that by 2020, Germany will need 2 million people to fill open jobs. Also, retiring workers are expected to drain the country's bank account because the government pays for their health care and other social services, or help for those in need.

The problem is harming many businesses, from high-tech electronics to nursing homes. There are simply not enough engineers, doctors, and teachers. In fact, as of 2011, Germany needs 12,000 doctors and 80,600 engineers.

"It's not easy finding qualified staff to take care of the elderly," says Dana Russow, who runs a nursing home in Berlin.

This automated Volkswagen storage tower in Wolfsburg, Germany, reflects Germany's economic growth in the 1990s.

WELCOMING FOREIGN WORKERS

Help is on the way, though. Years ago, Germany stopped foreign workers from coming into the country. Now, the German government is welcoming **immigrants**, foreigners who come to live there, from Eastern Europe. German officials hope that workers from Poland, the Czech Republic, Slovakia, Turkey, and other countries will fill the open jobs. The migration is an important sign of globalization.

In addition, the government is changing certain rules to help foreign doctors, engineers, and scientists find work. "We need different rules, rules that do justice to today's globalized world," says Education Minister Annette Schavan.

Currently, about 7 million of the 81 million people living in Germany are immigrants. Immigrants are evident in German cities, schools, and universities. Germany has become a society of numerous cultures. While the government is trying to integrate immigrants into society, many native Germans still do not welcome foreigners.

Turkish women in Berlin celebrate their culture in a traditional dance for May First festivities.

HOW WELCOME ARE IMMIGRANTS?

The government's "open border" policy has upset some Germans. They fear that immigrants will take their jobs and drive wages down. Some native Germans also want all immigrants to learn the German language. Meanwhile, many immigrants, especially Turkish workers, have been living in Germany for decades. They want to celebrate their own cultures. The government insists that immigrants accept Germany's way of life.

Also, people in Poland and other European countries worry that too many of their scientists and engineers will move to Germany. They fear it may create a "brain drain" in their countries.

Explore the Issue

1. **Analyze Causes** What are three reasons that Germany became so successful?

2. **Draw Conclusions** What are the tensions between immigrants and native Germans?

Japan

cars for the World

Japan prepares to export hundreds of cars all over the world at one of its many ports.

DISASTER RELIEF ACROSS THE GLOBE

Mackenzie Pitcock was about to leave Mobile, Alabama, for Japan when an earthquake and tsunami struck Japan on March 11, 2011. The disaster killed thousands of Japanese. Mackenzie, 16, living in Mobile, saw pictures of crushed cities and torn towns. "I knew I needed to do something," she said.

Mackenzie and other Alabama students sprang into action. They raised thousands of dollars to help the victims. When tornadoes ripped through Alabama that April, the Japanese returned the favor, sending relief.

Alabama and Japan have a special bond. That's because Alabama is home to several Japanese auto factories. These factories have created thousands of much-needed jobs in places such as Huntsville and Lincoln. The connection between Japan and Alabama is a prime result of globalization.

SWITCHING GEARS

Building cars has helped make Japan one of the world's richest countries. You can't go anywhere today without seeing a Japanese-built car. But that wasn't always so. At one time, American cars ruled the road. They were made from Pennsylvania steel and Ohio rubber. The cars were big, bright, and used a great deal of gas.

During the 1970s, gasoline shortages forced many Americans to rethink their ride. They abandoned their beloved Chevys and Fords and bought smaller, more fuel-efficient Japanese models. In no time, Japan became the world's largest carmaker.

Building cars is one of the earliest examples of globalization after World War II. The movement of products from one part of the world to another is a major aspect of globalization.

A Japanese auto company owns this Toyota factory in Huntsville, Alabama.

RISE TO THE TOP

That rise to the top began soon after Japan's defeat in World War II. At the time, the United States helped rebuild Japan's shattered economy, including its auto industry. In 1961, Japan **exported**, or sent for sale abroad, 10,000 vehicles for the first time. That number increased to 1 million in the early 1970s. Originally, Japanese cars had a poor reputation. However, good fuel economy, low prices, and improved quality helped raise sales quickly. Business was so good that in the 1980s, Japanese automakers built factories in the United States.

The payoff was huge. In 2008, Toyota muscled out General Motors to become the world's No. 1 carmaker, a title Toyota held until 2011. Japan's factories exported cutting edge technology. They excelled in cell phones, computers, and even robots for the home. Japan is now the world's third largest economy.

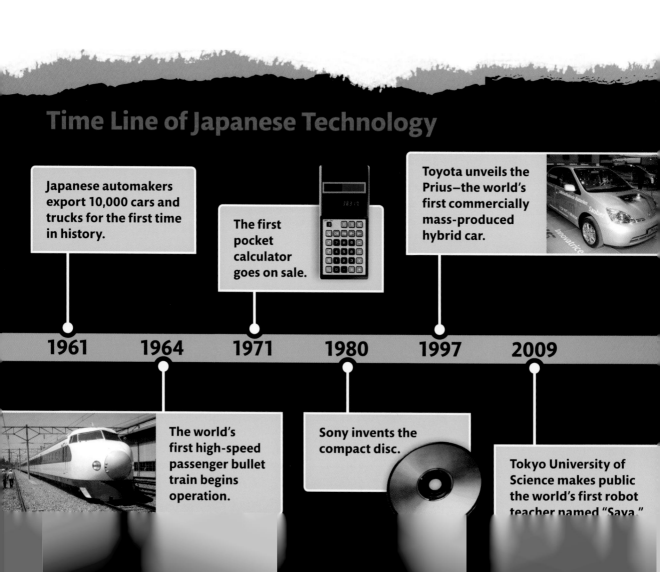

Time Line of Japanese Technology

Japanese automakers export 10,000 cars and trucks for the first time in history.

The first pocket calculator goes on sale.

Toyota unveils the Prius—the world's first commercially mass-produced hybrid car.

1961   **1964**   **1971**   **1980**   **1997**   **2009**

The world's first high-speed passenger bullet train begins operation.

Sony invents the compact disc.

Tokyo University of Science makes public the world's first robot teacher named "Saya."

PROTECTION CONNECTION

Japan was successful, in part, because its government limited foreign **imports**, or goods made in other countries. That policy, known as protectionism, gave Japanese companies an advantage over foreign competitors. In particular, Japan restricted the number of foreign cars coming into its country.

That restriction put foreign carmakers at a disadvantage. Countries such as the United States could not sell enough cars in Japan. U.S. car companies had to cut thousands of jobs. Because trade with Japan was so lopsided, South Korean automaker Hyundai refused to sell any more automobiles in Japan.

However, in some ways U.S. consumers benefited from the competition. The quality of U.S. cars improved. The Japanese created "hybrid" cars that use both gasoline and electricity. Finally, Japanese factories in the United States employed thousands of Americans.

This humanoid robot on the right sings and dances with real people at the Digital Contents Expo in Tokyo in 2010.

A CHANGING CULTURE

Because of Japan's success, many Japanese started to live better lives. Women entered the workforce. Both the standard of living and health care improved. Japanese people sent their children to college, traveled, and invested in countries abroad.

Yet problems surfaced. The Japanese slowly lost bits of their culture. Globalization led to more cultural trends that spread from one part of the world to another. Young people shunned traditional clothes in favor of American fashions. Ancient ways of writing were erased. Long-held traditions clashed with new ideas and customs brought from around the world.

Japanese workers, once guaranteed jobs for life, found themselves out of work. They lost their jobs in the 1990s when China started competing aggressively to sell products. To save money, Japanese firms cut thousands of jobs. Those who still had jobs worked long hours at low pay. Many of the unemployed became poor and homeless. Almost 20 million Japanese now live in poverty.

TIES ACROSS THE GLOBE

Despite the economic problems, Japan's car industry is still strong, as are the ties between Japan and the United States. In Lincoln, Alabama, 4,000 Americans work in a Honda factory, churning out 300,000 car engines and vehicles a year. Their employers are in Japan. The town of Lincoln prospers, as people have built homes and opened businesses. In 2010, motor vehicles were Alabama's top export.

The Honda factory shows how businesses from any country can now operate anywhere in the world. American companies also make and sell products all over the world. Globalization is tying the economies of countries more tightly together.

Explore the Issue

1. **Summarize** How did Japan become the world's top automaker?

2. **Analyze Effects** In what ways did the Japanese auto industry affect the United States?

A woman in a traditional kimono passes the modern Japanese stock market display, as new and old cultures live side by side in Tokyo.

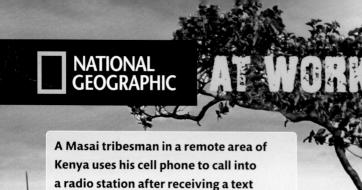

A Masai tribesman in a remote area of Kenya uses his cell phone to call into a radio station after receiving a text message through Ken Banks's innovation.

Ken Banks

&

Communication Technology for All

WHAT DID YOU SAY?

Globalization helps people around the world communicate with one another. That's what Ken Banks realized as he thought about how to help people living far away from cities all over the world.

When the rains come to the remote Cambodian village of Ta Reach, Sophana Pich [suh-FAN-nuh PIK] gets to work. Sophana helps people with malaria, a deadly disease carried by mosquitoes. In Ta Reach, Sophana usually diagnoses five to six cases each month. Not long ago, it took time for Sophana to communicate with doctors in Cambodia's capital, Phnom Penh [puh-NAHM PEN], about 93 miles away. No phone lines and no Internet connect Ta Reach to the capital. The delay meant that help could not arrive in time.

Ken Banks got the inspiration for FrontlineSMS while in South Africa.

Today, health care workers can communicate more quickly thanks to a computer software program introduced by Ken Banks, a National Geographic Emerging Explorer. "Before, it would take a month before this information was reported," Sophana says.

LINKING ACROSS LONG DISTANCES

We all take talking to our friends for granted. Some of us use cell phones, others text or tweet, still others send e-mails. However, in many rural areas, such communication is impossible. No one knows this better than Ken Banks.

When he was working in South Africa, Banks saw that people could not communicate over long distances. Just as in Ta Reach, parts of South Africa had no Internet service. Most of the phones in use are still very basic. They could not support the Internet even if there were Internet service. Banks wanted to find a way to help people in these areas to communicate. One day, as he sat watching a soccer game, he had an idea. What would happen, Banks wondered, if he built a system that used a cell phone network instead of the Internet?

The result was a computer program called FrontlineSMS. The software turns a cheap laptop and a cell phone into a text messaging communication center that does not require Internet access.

A village phone operator in Uganda shows off her cell phone, which she hires out for use one call or text at a time.

"Anyone can use this tool to solve a problem they see in the place where they live."—Ken Banks

TWO STEPS TO COMMUNICATION

How does FrontlineSMS work? First, the users download the free software. Then they simply attach a cable from the mobile phone to the computer. All that people need is one bar of mobile phone coverage to send their message. Using FrontlineSMS, a person can communicate with anyone on a contact list no matter how far away the other person is. "After downloading the free software online, you never need the Internet again," Banks says.

Banks's software has helped millions of people around the world. It saves time and lives. In Cambodia, Sophana can now report cases of malaria instantly to the government, which can respond right away. People living in the African country of Malawi are also receiving better health care. This happened because a college student brought hundreds of recycled phones and a laptop loaded with the FrontlineSMS.

"ALL I HAD WAS AN IDEA"

Banks is a scientist trained in social anthropology, the study of how people live. He also works in **conservation**, the saving of the environment. However, computer technology really excites Banks. Because of his new system, rural areas can get medicine. Doctors can treat patients who are hundreds of miles away. Farmers can find out current crop prices.

In addition to medicine and farming, Banks's system also helps people troubleshoot other technology problems in Africa. For example, he helped develop and share ways to get rid of kitchen waste using biogas digestors.

"Anyone can use this tool to solve a problem they see in the place where they live," Banks says. "We need to help people realize that if you care enough, you can do meaningful things without piles of money or expensive hardware. All I had was an idea."

Explore the Issue

1. Identify Problems Why couldn't people in remote regions communicate over long distances?

2. Identify Solutions How does Banks's tool solve communication problems in remote areas?

What Can I DO?

Catalog Where Products Are Made—and become a knowledgeable consumer

Your shoes, your computer, and your smartphone were probably made somewhere other than the United States. But do you know where? Research and catalog where different brands of the same product came from, and share what you learn with your class. You and your classmates will then become knowledgeable consumers.

IDENTIFY

- Pick any product, such as athletic shoes, televisions, or smartphones.

- Choose five brand names for that product on which to base your research.

- Create a simple database or spreadsheet to record the information from your research.

ORGANIZE

- Use the Internet and the library to find where each brand was made.

- Identify how each product arrived in the United States.

- Write a list of questions to ask about the path the product followed.

- Interview a store manager or clerk to see how each product arrived in the store.

These jeans took a long path through several countries to get to the consumer.

DOCUMENT

- Take your own photos or download photos of each brand.

- Identify the countries that made the parts of each brand and the country where the product was put together.

- Write a description comparing and contrasting where each brand was made, how it came to the United States, and its cost.

SHARE

- Create a map or a chart with arrows showing the route each brand took on its journey to the United States.

- Present to your classmates where and how each of the products was made and how it got to the store. Urge them to always consider where and how a product was made before buying.

Research & **WRITE**
Argumentative

Write an Argumentative Article

How do consumers make buying choices? Should Americans buy products that are "Made in America"? Write a paper arguing for or against a public awareness campaign to persuade Americans to purchase products made in the United States.

RESEARCH

Use the Internet, books, magazines, and newspapers to find support for your point of view. Make sure your sources are reliable. Look for the following:

- Several reasons that support your argument
- Costs or economic statistics that support your opinion
- Quotations and facts that support your opinion

As you do your research, be sure to take notes on note cards or on a computer.

DRAFT

Write the first draft of the article. It should be four paragraphs long.

- The first paragraph, or introduction, should introduce your opinion about a public campaign to "buy American."
- The following two paragraphs should develop your argument with clear reasons, relevant facts, definitions, and solid details. Use direct quotations or paraphrase the information and conclusions of others, such as economists, consumers, or sellers.
- In the fourth paragraph, provide a conclusion that reinforces your argument for or against a public campaign.

REVISE & EDIT

Look over your draft to make sure your argument is clearly stated and supported by the evidence. Revise the article to make it as persuasive as possible.

- Does the introduction state your opinion and grab the reader's attention?
- Did you include convincing facts?
- Are the supporting paragraphs focused on sound judgment and reasons that add weight to your opinion?
- Use transition words and phrases, along with strong verbs, to make your writing interesting, lively, and convincing.
- Make sure the quotations are accurate and the information is correct.
- Check your paper for spelling and punctuation.

PUBLISH & PRESENT

Combine your article with an article from a classmate who took the opposite point of view. Bind the articles together and create a cover for the published document. Copy the articles for your class. Have your classmates read both articles and vote on which one was more persuasive.

economy

natural resource

Common Market *n.*, an economic alliance of countries in the European Union that dropped trade barriers among its members

communist *adj.*, having a government with a social and economic philosophy that aims for a classless society and the absence of private property

conservation *n.*, an effort to protect the environment

democracy *n.*, a government in which power is in the hands of the people and exercised by their representatives

economy *n.*, a system of producing and distributing wealth

euro *n.*, the form of money used by most countries in the European Union

European Union (EU) *n.*, an economic and political association of countries in Europe

export *n.*, a good or product that is sent to another country for sale

globalization *n.*, the way countries use technology, communication, and transportation to connect to others

immigrant *n.*, a person who comes to a country to become a permanent resident

import *n.*, a good or product that is brought into a country for sale

natural resource *n.*, a valuable material that comes from the environment such as coal, oil, or gold

euro

export

globalization

INDEX

SKILLS